Pessimistic Persuasion 101

How to Talk Anyone out of Anything

By Richard Carey

Copyright 2017 by Richard Carey

Published by Make Profits Easy LLC

Profitsdaily123@aol.com

facebook.com/MakeProfitsEasy

Table of Contents

Introduction

Do you want to be able to talk anyone out of anything?

Persuasion is a unique art with which you can get people to do what you want. It is a wonderful way to get your way in the world and remain on top. However, it is not that hard to get people to do something. It is a little more difficult to get people to not do something. The art of pessimistic persuasion, or talking people out of doing things, is a unique topic that has barely been explored in the realm of persuasion and communication. Now you are about to learn this interesting art.

You may find that your loved one is about to do something. Maybe your significant other wants to break up with you and you want to keep him or her around. Maybe your boss wants to fire you, or your friend wants to date someone that you hate. Your child may decide not to go to college or your spouse may be considering a job that will force the entire family to move across the country, from your beloved home. Sometimes you will find that people want to make decisions that will negatively impact your life. For whatever reason, you will probably encounter plenty of situations where you want to get someone to *not* do what they want to do. You must persuade them out of whatever action or decision they are about to make.

Pessimistic persuasion is not always self-serving. Sometimes, it is for the greater good of the people that you love. It is a great technique to learn, especially if you are a parent. Often children make screwball decisions or huge mistakes in their lives. They refuse to listen to their parents. If you know how to persuade someone not to do something, however, you can prevent your children from a lot of heartache. You can also take care of yourself and prevent people from making decisions that hurt you. Knowing pessimistic persuasion will enable you to prevent fights and break-ups, keep your job, and talk your friends out of bad moves.

In order to accomplish pessimistic persuasion, you first must understand a lot about persuasion and common persuasion methods. We will touch on that in Chapter 1. From there, you will learn all about how to apply those principles to talking anyone out of anything. The concept behind pessimistic persuasion is the same as regular persuasion: You want to make someone do what you want, which in this case involves not doing what they want. You must provide a valid argument and present yourself as an authority. You must have their trust and liking. Finally, you must show them how they will benefit by not taking the action that you don't want them to take.

But pessimistic persuasion is a little bit different in application. You are trying to convince someone to change his or her mind. You must present a very convincing argument that really appeals to his or her intelligence and makes him or her reticent to take the undesired action.

There are many elements of pessimistic persuasion. You may just use a simple argument to get your spouse to go to a different restaurant for dinner. Or you might subliminally influence someone to not date your worst enemy. Or you may even train someone over time with operant conditioning to not perform a behavior or action that you hate. Pessimistic persuasion can be as basic and simple or as complex and advanced as you want it to be. You can accomplish amazing things with pessimistic persuasion, as you bend others to your will.

Of course, pessimistic persuasion can be used for evil. You can intentionally use it to hurt others. If you choose to use pessimistic persuasion for these purposes, you are doing it at your own risk and on your own conscience. Understand that pessimistic persuasion does not have to be evil. You can use it only for good.

Also remember that pessimistic persuasion is best used only when someone is fully committed to a decision that you don't support. Sometimes it is easier and better to just ask someone not to do something. Directness is usually better in relationships. Too much persuasion can border on manipulation or even emotional abuse and can lose its power if overused. If he or she refuses to comply with your request, then you can start to apply pessimistic persuasion to get your way.

Make sure that you really want to change your subject's mind before you use pessimistic persuasion. These persuasive methods are incredibly effective. They will most likely work. Therefore, if you have second thoughts, you should not use these methods. There is no turning back once you apply them.

In regular persuasion, stealth is usually advised. There are ways to be stealthy in pessimistic persuasion, which we certainly cover in this book. But sometimes it is not always possible to be stealthy when talking someone out of something. In the very nature of this persuasion, you must reveal your stance and your disapproval. That is OK. You can recover and save face by showing your subject how much you care and how you are only doing this out of concern for his or her well-being. The fact that you are being persuasive should not be a source of conflict if you present it from this angle.

Now are you ready to become extremely persuasive and to be able to talk people out of anything? Then read on! You will be an expert by the time you finish this book.

Chapter 1: The Basic Art of Persuasion

Before we delve into this fascinating topic of pessimistic persuasion, we should first touch on the basics of persuasion. You will need to know these in order to understand the more advanced pessimistic persuasion methods that we cover in the subsequent chapters.

Persuasion is a deeply studied topic that has been studied by many psychologists and social scientists. There is a wealth of proven information out there about how to properly and effectively persuade someone. You can trust science to bring you accurate information about how to act to get people to do what you want.

Maslow's Hierarchy of Needs

One of the best ways to persuade someone to do (or not do) something is to show him how he will benefit by doing (or not doing) it. People act on a reward principle, meaning they will only do things that benefit them somehow. You must prove how something will benefit a person first.

Maslow's Hierarchy of Needs shows you what people usually really want and need in life. You can figure out how someone may benefit from something by picking a need from the Hierarchy of Needs. Understand that any need that you can satisfy in exchange for getting what you want will help you appeal to people. However, for the best results in persuasion, you want to find what your subject really wants and target that. He won't agree to do something for you if you are only offering to satisfy a need that he has already met.

Maslow's Hierarchy of Needs is a pyramid that lists peoples' needs, ranked from most important to least important. These are inherent needs that all people share. At the very bottom of the pyramid, which is the most important, are physiological needs, such as food and water. Then there is the need for safety, love, and security. Next comes the need for belonging to a group of people, such as having friends. There is the need for esteem and pride from your accomplishments. At the very tiptop of the pyramid is the need for achieving one's potential and fulfilling one's purpose in life.

Find out which of these needs someone really craves and how they can get it by doing what you want. Then promise the person the reward he or she will really love. You can spot what someone craves by what he talks about a lot or seems to long for. A person who wants to belong to a crowd at work might eat lunch alone while gazing longingly at his co-workers who are all eating together. A person who wants praise and affirmation for his accomplishments may seem irritated when no one acknowledges his work or may get competitive and try to take all the credit for everything that he does on a team. Finally, a person who always talks about women or men and dating is probably looking for a companion.

Cialdini's Six Principles of Influence

One of the major researchers in this field is the esteemed Dr. Robert Cialdini, who composed the book *Influence: The Psychology of Persuasion,* from which we get Cialdini's Six Principles of Influence. The Six Principles of Influence are essential for anyone to know who is interested in learning the art of persuasion.

The first principle is reciprocity. This is where you do something for someone, knowing that he will reciprocate the favor in some way. Make people feel like they owe you and they will be more inclined to do what you want. Do little favors for people to get them in your debt. Don't mention that you consider them to be in your debt. Simply call on them for a favor later and if they refuse, mention, "Well, I did such-and-such for you a year ago. Think you could return the favor now please?"

The second principle is commitment and consistency. People love to be consistent and they tend to stick to what they know. This means that you are more likely to get someone to do what you want if that person is already doing something similar or invested in a cause that you represent. This is the principle that lies behind customer loyalty, for example. Companies can get people to buy more from them once they establish a trust and commitment to the brand.

The third principle is social proof. This is basically where you get people to do something because it is a trend. You show people that others like whatever you are selling or proposing. This makes them want to join in and get it too. Having endorsements from respectable people, such as doctors or scientists, can make you seem like you are much loved by authorities and that you are a trustworthy brand. Walking around with lots of friends can make you seem like a likable person, which makes others want to please you by doing things for you. Having a friend talk you up to someone can score you a date more easily than if you just try to talk yourself up to the person.

The fourth principle is authority. You want to show that you have authority. This is a big one in pessimistic persuasion, since you are trying to get people to believe in your point of view. People will obey those with authority. Establishing yourself as an authority by posting your degrees and qualifications or speaking knowledgably about a topic can get others to trust your word and do what you say. If you are not an authority, then get an authority figure to back you, someone with an impressive title like "Dr."

The fifth principle is to get people to like you. This is called liking. With liking, you can influence people if they like you as a person. You want to be sympathetic, friendly, and kind to others. Remember details like when their birthdays are. When people talk to you, listen and ask questions to show that you are interested, even if you are not at all. This will make people like you. Then they will consider you a friend and do things for you. Being physically attractive and investing in your appearance and hygiene also helps with this.

Finally, the sixth principle is scarcity. Scarcity is where you pressure people into doing something because they think they are short on time. This is why ads will say, "Limited supply! Act fast or supplies will run out! This deal won't last!" Make someone feel like they have to make a decision fast. This pressure will make them say yes before the supply runs out or you move on and extend an offer to someone else.

Amplification Hypothesis

When you use the Amplification Hypothesis, you are using your attitude to sway someone's opinion on a matter. If you express certainty about something, the other person becomes convinced that his attitude is right. He sticks to it. If you express uncertainty, his conviction begins to fade and soften. He is not so sure of himself anymore.

Getting someone to do what you want can be as simple as acting enthusiastic about a decision that he makes. Your enthusiasm reassures him that he is in the right. He will be more likely to stick to the decision that you like if you provide emotional support and approval.

If you disagree with someone, just express a little doubt. You will probably be able to change his opinion, or at least soften his conviction. For instance, if he says that he is going to do something, ask him, "Are you sure that is a good idea?" Seem very doubtful and disapproving. He will probably defend his decision, but he will start to feel doubt too. Don't just argue with someone and tell him why you are doubtful, as he will be able to justify or reason with each of your reasons. Simply express doubt and disapproval to shake his conviction.

Conversion Theory

In the conversion theory, being part of a minority can actually give you more influence over the majority. The one voice that speaks out with an unpopular opinion or attitude can have the hugest effect on others. The minority can often sway the majority and gain favor.

So if you want to change someone's mind, maybe expose him or her to the minority opinion. Speak out with what you believe in, especially if you hold an unpopular opinion. You will shock others and gain more followers and assenters than you thought possible.

Information Manipulation Theory

To be persuasive, you can try to break one of the four main conversational maxims, or governing rules. By doing this, you can make someone doubt his own mind or begin to accept what you have to say. Breaking a conversational maxim will alarm the other person because it disrupts the expected order of things.

There are four maxims:

- Quantity: You give all of the information expected.
- Quality: You tell the truth.

- Relation: You speak about something that is relevant to the conversation.
- Manner: You speak in a lucid way that the other person can understand.

So if you give a short and evasive answer, avoid telling the truth, change the subject, or speak in a hard to comprehend way, you can sway the other person's opinion. You can make him wonder what is really going on. You can also show him that you are upset by his opinion or decision, which may make him change it. When you disrupt one of the conversational maxims, you gain some persuasive power over your subject.

Priming

Priming is where you get someone to think a certain way by telling him certain words or exposing him to stimuli. You "prime" him to think what you want by exposing him to an outside stimuli that makes him think of what you desire. For instance, if you want your friend to choose an Italian restaurant for dinner, you might expose him to Italian words, pictures of pasta, or even the scent of Italian cooking. He starts thinking "Italian" and later he picks the restaurant you want without even realizing why he has picked it.

Sleeper Effect

The Sleeper Effect is the concept that a minimally persuasive message will gain persuasiveness over time as a person gains distance from the source. For example, a used car salesman might not seem very credible at first as he tells you what kind of car to buy. But after you leave the lot, the message about the ideal car will gain significance in your mind and you may become swayed about what kind of car to buy. Later, you pick the car that he suggested, without realizing why. You can apply this concept by telling people an opinion and then letting the message sink in over time.

Yale Attitude Change Approach

Your attitude really affects how persuasive you are. You need to speak first and come across as an authoritative source. You also need to appear confident, like you know what you are talking about. Having an excited and positive attitude is also important in getting other people to want to believe your opinion or follow your lead into a decision.

Ultimate Terms

Specific words carry more power than others. Using really strong language can impress someone into believing what you are saying. You can make impression with words that imply God, such as blessings or obedience. You can also use devil terms, which imply disgust, hatred, sin, and eternal damnation. Finally, you can use charismatic terms which emphasize values like freedom, hard work, and emotional awards for doing the right thing. All of these terms appeal strongly to someone's senses, causing that person to become more inclined to pay attention to you and take the action that you prescribe.

For instance, to get someone to change jobs, you might compare his current job to Hell. As he thinks about it, he will start to notice more and more examples of how horrible his job is. Your comparison to Hell will make him focus on why his job is like Hell and he will begin to think of his job in only negative terms. Meanwhile, compare the job you are offering him to Heaven or use charismatic terms. Tell him how his new job will help him help more people or make more important friends in the business network. Show him how his ideals fit with the new company's. This makes him focus on what he can gain from the new position and he will think of it only in positive terms.

Similarly, you can use this tactic in marketing. Tell people how your product or service will give them emotional awards, such as more friends and more dates. Use charismatic terms to make them want to purchase what you are selling because they associate your product or service with the ultimate in success and popularity.

Offer Rewards and Focus on Gain

People like to gain rewards when they do something. Most people operate on a reward principle, where they only do something when they know that they will get something they want in exchange. You can't get a person to do what you want or to buy something just because. People don't respond well to "just because." Rather, people need to see a reason to do something for you.

A good way to accomplish this form of reward motivation is to convince someone that he will gain something by doing what you want. You want to make him think that by doing something for you, he will receive a rich reward that will benefit him handsomely. Play up the reward that you can give him in exchange for his cooperation.

Speak only in terms of gain. You don't want to say things like, "You will stop doing this" or "You will lose weight." Instead, speak of how "You will gain healthier habits" or "You will gain health." When you phrase things in terms of gain, the reward seems prettier and more desirable. Therefore, your subject will be more enthusiastic about gaining that reward.

Terms of gain are so essential in persuasion. You want to emphasize the positive at all times. Play up your reward and talk about how much you have to offer. It is OK to promise the moon. The more you sell yourself, the more persuasive you become. The subject does not have to know whether he will really gain these results or not. He just has to think that he will and want to try his luck.

You should also focus on figuring out what your subject might really want. If you want someone to go to a party with you so that you are not alone, and your friend doesn't want to go but he talks about how much he hates being single, promise him that he will meet more girls if he goes to the party with you. If you want to sell a weight loss supplement, tell your potential customers about how much sexier they will feel when they take your pill and how many more dates they will get. Talk about how they can get a revenge body that will make their exes jealous.

However, you should not exclusively focus on gain in all circumstances. Sometimes, it is OK to point out what someone stands to lose. If you can show him what he stands to lose by making a bad decision, you may be able to scare him into reason.

Remove Your Ego

When persuading someone, you can't just force yourself onto him. You must approach him in a way that appeals to him. This means removing your ego from the equation and focusing on what the other person wants. Show him what benefits him. Leave yourself out of the discussion; no one will be persuaded to do something for you if you just talk about how you will benefit.

The very act of persuasion is a selfish one. You want something and you want to get someone to do it for you. Your motives are not altruistic. But generally, you want to pretend as if they are. Act as if your interests are purely selfless and you want the best for someone else. Your own ego and your own needs only get in the way of persuasion. You know what you want, but hide that from the other person, because no one wants to slave away just for your benefit.

Challenge Someone

A lot of people are very competitive. They love to win and they love to be right. You can use that to your advantage by challenging someone to do something. Use reverse psychology and say something like, "I bet you couldn't do this if you tried." Or say, "I bet he's better than you at making sales." Your subject will be upset that you don't believe in him and he will thus rise to the challenge. This motivational persuasion method works best with people who have big egos or competitive natures and who like to compete and win.

Alternatively, you can let someone know that you believe in him. Push him to please you by telling him, "I know you can do this." He will have his doubts about his abilities, but he will not want to let you down since you believe in him so much. Therefore, he will do what you want to make you continue to believe in him by doing what you want perfectly. Positive reinforcement and encouragement works especially well with people who suffer from low self-esteem or who aim to please others to gain favor.

Often, when you push someone to do their best and encourage them to step out of their comfort zone, he will want to succeed. He will want to please you just to satiate his own ego. Rising to a challenge and succeeding is a great ego boost for people; they will want to do it just to make themselves happy. Use that to your advantage and challenge people to rise above what they are used to. Get them to succeed by pushing them. It is OK to challenge people and get them to go above and beyond their current abilities.

Yes Track

Get a person saying "yes" to make him more likely to tell you yes. If you get someone on a yes track, then he will keep saying yes until he agrees to what you want. It is a glitch in the brain that causes this and you can exploit it.

Start by asking him questions that he is likely to say yes to. "It's nice today, isn't it?" "You like this car?" "Are you feeling great today?" "Are you ready for the weekend?" Once you get him saying yes again and again, finally pop your pressing question. He will most likely say yes to it.

Chapter 2: Convince People that You are Right

The biggest concept that lies behind talking people out of things is convincing them that you are right. When you convince someone that you are right, he or she will listen to you. He will believe you when you say, "Don't do that."

Convincing someone that you are right is a little different than regular persuasion, but it uses many of the same principles. In regular persuasion, you are trying to convince someone that it is a good idea to do a favor for you, to buy your product or service, to donate money to your cause, or to assist you in reaching a goal. You are trying to appeal to someone to get him to do what he may not do. But when you are trying to win an argument, you are trying to persuade someone to change his point of view in favor of yours. You are trying to get him to see things in life differently and to accept that he is wrong and you are right. This is not an easy feat, especially since people like to be right and they like to hold onto their ideas.

That does not mean that it is an impossible feat, however. You simply have to appeal to someone and make him like you and trust you. Then you must show him how you are right. You don't want to focus on proving him wrong, as this will just anger him and make him resistant to your ideas. Rather, show him that you are more correct and he would benefit by adopting your point of view. You want to be tactful and diplomatic, but also firm and extremely convincing.

When you get someone to see that you are right, then he will hopefully adopt your reasoning. This can make him change his mind about a decision that he has made. Thus, you managed to talk him out of something.

Here are some tips on how to do this.

Approach at the Right Time

In persuasion, timing is everything. You want to approach your subject when it is a good time. He will not be the most receptive to your messages when he is preoccupied, stressed, busy, just waking up, or otherwise engaged. Don't talk to him when he is with friends or dates. Don't talk to him when he is on the phone or at work. If he appears to be in a bad mood, or has just had a bad experience, don't hit him with your argument.

Instead, set up a time that is good for him for a talk. Ask him, "When can we talk? I really need to talk to you. Please set aside some time to chat with me." Let him pick a time and come to you. If the matter is urgent, you can put some pressure on him to set aside time soon, but don't inundate him with demands on his time.

When you speak to him, first make sure that he feels comfortable. This keeps him from getting defensive. Make sure that he is seated and at a comfortable temperature. Offer him something warm to drink, like coffee, because warm beverages can make him subconsciously associate you with warmth and thus he will like you more in that moment.

Start the conversation in a pleasant and friendly manner. Don't be rude, defensive, or confrontational or you will lose the battle before you even begin it.

Never say "You're Wrong"

Never, under any circumstances, tell the person that you are persuading the words, "You are wrong." It is a simple matter of pride: people hate being told that they are wrong. When you say that someone is wrong, you hurt his ego and put him on the defensive. He stops seeing reason and instead becomes hell-bent on convincing you of his rightness. He becomes committed to proving you wrong and himself right for the sake of his ego. In addition, he becomes hurt and associates your opinion with the unpleasant experience of being told that he is wrong. Thus, he will never listen to you or come around to your way of reasoning.

It is far better to tell someone, "I see why you think that." Even if you don't see why at all, pretend that you do. Let him know that his argument is valid and that he is not necessarily wrong. But then say something like, "But did you consider this?" Point out some facts that he may have not considered. Lay out your argument politely and tactfully without once telling him that he is wrong.

Do Not Argue

Arguing is never a good thing to do. Really, it is just a huge waste of time. When you argue with someone, you put him on the defensive. This makes him resistant to what you are saying and causes him to disregard your words as he thinks of words that will win the argument.

Never start an argument with someone. Keep your voice calm and rational and approach the discussion as a friendly debate, not an unpleasant or ferocious argument. If he keeps trying to argue, just say, "I'm not trying to argue here."

It is also helpful to stop thinking in terms of winning or losing. When you approach a discussion from the standpoint that you must win, then you will naturally turn it into an argument. Rather, think of it as a chance to convince him of your point of view. You will then work harder to present a convincing rationalization rather than trying to win.

Do Not Become Defensive

You may hate it when someone does not just blindly accept your point of view and change their minds for you. As someone begins to disagree with you, you may become both insulted and eager to prove him wrong. You go on the defensive and lose your ability to rationalize. Being defensive causes you to lose all credibility. You blow your chances at talking him out of a decision or deciding that you are right.

People have their own free will. Therefore, a person will often see things differently from you and take a different approach to life. Accept this fact. Remain patient as you try to present your reasoning and convince him to see things your way. Don't get defensive. Your ego needs to rest during this time, or it will make you lose your subject.

Let Him Think It's His Idea

People love following their own ideas. They are not so receptive to the ideas and advice of others. So when you want to talk someone out of something, just be the listener as he discusses his plans or decisions. Don't talk too much. Point out little things that he is forgetting in his logic so that he starts thinking of the solution that you want. Let him think that it is his own idea. Then he will actually do what you want.

Shift Focus from the Problem to the Solution

If you shift someone's focus from his problem to the solution, you accomplish two things. First, you make him feel that you are focused more on solving his problems than just letting him ruminate in them, which makes him feel that you are interested in helping him solve his problems and that you possess a lot of wisdom so he should listen to you. You also help him shift his focus from ruminating to working with you to find a solution. This is the easiest way to get him to think that the solution you want him to come up with his own idea.

One way to shift his focus is to ask, "Would it be helpful if...?" or "Have you considered trying...?" Start sentences this way to make him more receptive to the message. Once you ask him a question, let him think about the answer. He will think that the answer is his own idea and he will be thrilled that he just solved a problem on his own. Meanwhile, you got him to do what you wanted.

You could also say "What if?" to get him to consider your idea. He will start brainstorming and will springboard himself into your desired line of thinking. You can kick the brainstorming off with a simple suggestion that leads in the path you want him to follow, but let him do the rest of the work.

Finally, consider finding out what he really thinks and what problems he foresees with his decision. Ask him, "What do you see could be a problem here?" Let him think of problems and cause him to doubt his decision.

Express Sympathy and Understanding

When convincing someone that you are right, you don't want to come across overbearing or rude. You also don't want to seem like you don't understand. If you are not understanding, you will alienate your subject and make him think that you are wrong simply because you don't see his side of things. By being sympathetic and understanding, you make him feel warmer. You make him think that he is wrong since you understand but you still don't think that he is right.

Also show that you understand by acknowledging what he says without telling him that he is wrong or talking over him. Nod and say, "Yes, I understand." Maybe even follow his train of thought to show that you are on the same page as him. Say things like, "I can see why you feel that way."

It can be helpful to reiterate what someone says to indicate that you are listening and that you fully understand. Repeat back what he says but say it a little differently. Paraphrase.

Make lots of sympathy sounds and nod your head frequently to show that you are actively listening. Maybe ask him some involved questions to further show your interest. Let him do most of the talking as you do most of the listening.

Dramatize Your Ideas

The more dramatic and climatic you make your ideas seem, the more likely someone is to idealize them and follow them. You want to make your ideas seem sky high and wonderful. Hold people to your high standards.

It is all about presentation. A huge part of persuasion is being appealing to your subject by presenting what you want in a way that he will like. Therefore, you want to appeal to his wants, his needs, and his ideals. You can play your ideas up to seem lofty and somehow better than what he currently believes in. Make your ideas seem like something that will better him as a person and get him closer to his ideas.

Tell your subject how your new business model will launch him into six-figure success, for example, so that he buys into the model. Or tell someone that they are better than what they currently believe in so that they accept your loftier ideals and uphold your beliefs.

Show Him Why You're Right

You won't show him that you're right just by telling him that he is wrong. Rather, you show him that you are right by genuinely proving to him that there is logic in what you are saying and that he will benefit by coming around to your point of view. Focus on what he will gain by coming around to your standpoint, not what he will lose by doing what he wants. Point out real-life reasons and examples of why you are right. If you can illustrate what you are saying with stories about other people or actions, then definitely do so. You want to drive the point home.

Also, bolster your opinion's relevance by showing him how it actually applies to his life. Give him concrete examples of how he will gain things that he really wants by doing what you say rather than what he wants. Scare him into thinking that he won't get those things with his decision.

Get Him to Wonder Why He is Saying No to You

If you get him to wonder why he is refusing to following your ideology, then he will start to doubt his own logic and consider following yours. You must make him start to question himself. Get him to think, "I may be wrong and he/she may be right. Why won't I listen?"

The best way to do this is to present him with *logos*. Logos is one of Aristotle's appeals and it refers to basic logic. If you are presenting someone with sound logic and don't appear to be manipulating him for any reason, then he has no reason not to listen to you. Appeal to his logic and ask him if he really thinks this is a good idea. Shake up his conviction in his choice by showing him how illogical it is.

You can also use *pathos* and appeal to his emotions. Remind him of how close you two used to be and show him that you miss him to keep him from moving away, for instance. Show him how he will regret it and all the things he will miss out on if he does what you don't want him to do.

Finally, there is *ethos*, Aristotle's third appeal. You want to appeal to his sense of ethos by coming across as an authority that he should listen to. Tell him that you have had similar life experiences and you know what he is about to go through so that he believes you. Use credible sources, such as psychologists or doctors, to get him to hear reason. Do whatever it takes to make him want to believe you. He will refuse to believe you if you don't seem to be credible or to know what you are talking about. If you show him that you have a very real reason for wanting him to change his mind, he just might.

Make Him feel Guilty for Saying No to You

If you want him to say yes, then ask for what you want second. When he says no to you the first time, he will feel a bit bad about it. So suggest a compromise. He will want to say yes to you so when he hears the compromise, he will feel that he should say yes to avoid letting you down further.

Therefore, if you really want something, ask him something that he will have to say no to. After he says no, ask for what you really want. He will feel that it is more reasonable than the first request and he will want to say yes anyway. For instance, if you want a raise, ask him for a huge amount. He will say no but he will probably feel bad. Then suggest the amount that you really want. It will seem better and he will want to oblige you.

Use We Terms

When you are trying to persuade someone, you want to use "we" terms. These terms facilitate the sense that the two of you are in this together and accomplishing something together. It makes the other person feel like he must make decisions with you since you are a team. Your words will bear more weight as a result.

"We" encourages cooperation. It elevates you from some person giving orders to a partner or teammate. People like that and will try to work with you since they don't like being alone. Avoid using lots of "I" terms because then you seem like you are only serving your own interests. Meanwhile, "you" terms can sound demanding or accusatory. It is far better to say something like, "We should do this," as opposed to saying, "I think you should do this."

Appear Confident and Sure of Yourself

When you are trying to convince someone that you are right, then you need to appear right. You can't be stuttering and showing that you lack confidence and conviction if you want to make someone believe what you have to say. Therefore, change your speech to be very confident. Use big words and talk fast. Talk with your hands. Don't stutter or falter or say things like "I don't know." Avoid laughing nervously or betraying nervous ticks. Establish ethos by appearing to believe in yourself wholeheartedly and expecting everyone else to believe you too.

If you are cocky and sure of yourself, you can gain others' trust. After all, how could you be so sure of yourself on the outside if you weren't on the inside? This is what people will think, anyway. Even if you are unsure of yourself, pretend to be an expert. Pretend to be totally sure of who you are and what you are saying.

You also want to appear warm and open. Don't cross your arms or legs. Don't keep your body turned. Don't avoid eye contact. Appear approachable and like you have nothing to hide by looking your subject in the eye, giving him a firm handshake, keeping your body language open, and standing directly before him. These gestures will assure him that you mean well and that you have nothing to hide. He will trust you more and thus believe you more.

Also make sure that you stay consistent. Your body language, your words, and your facial expression all need to match. If you are telling someone that you are sad, for instance, don't be smiling and laughing. Don't say you support the Republicans and then turn around and say that you are a registered Democrat. You are only credible and believable if you are consistent in your words and actions. Never underestimate the power of nonverbal communication, either.

What you don't say speaks volumes, so make sure that is consistent as well while you are persuading someone.

Appeal to His Image

Most people care a lot about how they look to others. So if you want to convince someone to listen to you, beg him to consider how his decision will make him appear to others. "What do you think this will make your mother think? What will your friends think? How will you ever be employable after this?" are the types of questions you can ask him to make him wonder how his image will be impacted. If you can make him fear for his image, then he may just change his mind.

A lot of people want to fit in. So you can use that to appeal to him. Tell him how he will be the odd one out and ask him if he minds that. Don't appear confrontational as you say this. Instead, act like you are just asking an innocent question. It will get him thinking about how his decision might alienate him. Then he will want to change his mind so that he can keep fitting in. You can use this to convince him to adopt your reasoning, too, by telling him that he will fit in and appear cool if he does what you want. Remember that you should focus on gain more than loss, so you can use the gain of coolness and popularity to motivate him to adopt your point of view.

On the other hand, you can use the minority opinion to influence him. Offering an unpopular opinion can have a big impact on his thinking. He will be more likely to listen to the minority than the majority.

You can also appeal to other things that he cares about, such as being loved or having money. Figure out what he really cares about and determine how to make him see that his decision might ruin that for him. This will scare him into listening to you. He will trust that you are the voice of reason, trying to protect him from losing everything that he cares about.

How do you find out what he cares about? Look at the clues he provides you. If he talks about his kids a lot and has pictures of them on his desk at work, for example, you can use appeals to his kids to motivate him. Say things like, "Don't you want your kids to look up to you? They will if you change your mind." If he is really into golf, talk him out of moving to a new community by pointing out that there are no great golf courses there. If he wants recognition at work and is always kissing the boss's butt, you should offer him favor with the boss and say, "Our boss will love you if you do this for me!"

Chapter 3: The Art of Dissuasion

Dissuasion is the process of persuading someone to change his course of action or to change his mind about a decision. The art of dissuasion is another name for pessimistic persuasion.

In the previous chapters we have discussed how to influence someone. Now let's get into the very exact application of using those concepts to talk someone out of something. You will learn how to convince someone not to do something, which is the entire point of pessimistic persuasion.

Before you even begin using the methods outlined in this book, you must keep two very important facts in mind. These facts are the keys to pessimistic persuasion. The first key fact is that you cannot argue with someone until you win. This is not an effective way to get your way at all. You catch more flies with honey. Remember that.

The second fact is that you must keep your goal in mind. If you lose sight of it, then you won't be able to focus on your subject and getting him to not do something. Always focus on the goal and the action or behavior that you want to avoid. Work hard toward that goal. Don't let other things distract you. If you have other things that you want to change about a person or multiple goals, don't let them get in the way. Just focus on one thing at a time. Attempting to change too much about a person will inevitably lead to failure. The person will become uncomfortable with your pushiness and will pull away and resist you to protect himself.

When selecting a goal to focus on, you want to find what is most important to you. The other things that you want to change can wait. You can even let go of your desire to change someone too much. Doing so is never a good idea. Just find the one thing that you really don't want him to do and concentrate on that. Stick by your goal until you reach your desired results.

Now let's explore the methods you can use to talk people out of stuff!

Frame a Loss

When you frame a loss, you are convincing someone that he stands to lose a lot if he follows through with his proposed action. You can convince him to not do what he is planning if you can scare him out of it. Show him what he stands to lose and the huge risks associated with his proposed action.

People are very influenced by fear. They hate losing things. While persuasion typically works by focusing on gain and positives, it is not so in pessimistic persuasion. To get someone to change his mind about a decision, you will usually have greater success framing a loss than a gain. You will be able to scare him out of his decision once he sees that his decision will bring him losses that he may not be able to recover from.

If you know someone well, then you will know what he cares about. Show him how his decision or action will take away or ruin what he loves. Scare him out of the decision.

When it comes to talking a stranger out of something, you might try to find things that he cares about. It may be hit or miss at first. Search his person for clues. Let's use a few examples. Say your subject is trying to commit suicide and you must talk him out of it. You don't know him at all. You can try to hit different points and ask him if he really wants to leave behind his children or his spouse. Ask him if he is really willing to never wake up again and never see another sunrise or sunset. You can check his phone or wallet to find out if he has family or pets that he loves, then ask him if he wants to leave them all behind.

Or say you are trying to get your boss to make a safer and smarter decision for the company. You know that he cares about the company's welfare and money. How could he not? So ask him if he is really willing to jeopardize his fortune and maybe wind up in bankruptcy.

Prepare for Contradictions

When someone makes a decision, he is probably not just making it for no reason at all. He has most likely done some thinking and put some time into the decision. He has thought of potential problems with his decision and he has probably come up with solutions. In addition, he has found ways to justify himself and defend his decision, especially if he knows that his loved ones or other people will raise objections. Therefore, you need to enter the discussion with him prepared for contradictions. For every point you bring up, he will have a counter argument.

You want to think of his reasoning and his potential contradictions. Think of tight arguments against them. Map out the discussion ahead of time and think of ways that it could go. Be prepared.

Of course, you cannot always be one hundred percent prepared. Sometimes, you will be surprised by an argument that your subject makes. In this case, just think fast. If you can't think of a counter argument, move on. Say, "You are right, but please think of the other things that you stand to lose."

Make Your Subject Feel Powerful

People have power and free will over their own lives. Respecting that fact, or at least pretending to, is a great way to make someone feel better about his relationship with you. He then becomes more willing to listen to you. Let him know that you respect his power to make his own decisions. Tell him that you want him to consider making a change to his decision for the betterment of everyone, including himself. You want to do this in a respectful way, appealing to his sense that he is in control. Phrase it like you are putting in a request. Don't ever bark commands at someone or act like you are in control, because you both know that you really are not. If you were really in control, then you wouldn't need pessimistic persuasion.

When you tell your subject that this is his decision, you make him feel like you are not trying to control him. This softens his eagerness to resist you to preserve his independence. He will become more open to your ideas if you phrase it like a request that you want him to consider, rather than a command or an order.

Think of how you would speak to your boss. You wouldn't dare tell him what to do, would you? Now approach your persuasion subject in this manner. Put in your request but don't tell him what to do. Present your evidence and frame a loss. Ask him, "Please rethink this." Don't tell him to actually rethink it or he will shut down and become resistant to you out of pride.

It may be helpful to use terms like: "I hope you consider this. Thank you for talking with me about this." "Please think about this and about what I said. I hope you make the best decision." "We can think of something better than this if you would just reconsider."

Be Prepared to Agree...on Some Things

You do not want to agree with someone too much if you are trying to talk him out of something. Obviously, you disagree with his decision and want to redirect him. However, if you agree a little bit on some things, you will come across as a friend rather than an opponent in an argument. He will become more receptive to your reason when he realizes that you are on his side and that you understand where he is coming from.

Acknowledge that he is right. The more you do this, the less on guard he will feel around you. Then, suggest, "I think that you are right about most things. But have you considered this? We should consider brainstorming a different solution." Or say something like, "I think you are right. But what if..." and bring up a valid and possible scenario that will frame a loss or propose some reason to him.

You don't want to give in too much. But if you don't give in at all, you will lose him in the argument. You will become obvious about your insistence at being right, which will make him stop listening to you. Therefore, you want to be careful and only disagree with him on a few points. Give him a few inches and he will probably give you a few feet.

Be Prepared to Compromise

You want him to do one thing. He wants to do the opposite. Your interests clash. In this case, maybe you should not expect him to meet you all the way. Instead, settle for halfway. Allow him to get a little bit of what he wants while you get a little bit of what you want. As long as you can talk him out of one action, that is probably good enough. You don't have to get him to do what you want all of the time. Just get him not to do what you don't want.

Therefore, you need to be prepared to compromise. You can't go into pessimistic persuasion expecting to win everything. This is about talking someone out of something, not winning. Be willing to budge on your resolve and you will have better luck talking someone out of something.

Similarly, while dissuading someone, you want to compliment him from time to time. Let him feel that you trust his decision-making and that you don't think he is stupid. That will make him more receptive to your message. He will think that you are looking out for him, not criticizing him. If you are always telling him that he is wrong, he will assume that you just don't believe in his judgment and that you are trying to control him. He will become more resistant to you. So take the opposite approach and kill him with kindness. Make him feel good about himself and make him think that you care. If you don't actually feel this way, then fake it.

Speak Fast

You want to speak fluidly and quickly, in a natural manner. When you do this, you seem like you really know what you are talking about. You also seem like you don't have some sort of exterior motive. Speaking fast denotes knowledge, wisdom, and confidence. If you speak unnaturally, you seem to be hiding something or struggling to think of what to say.

You will also seem more trustworthy if you speak knowledgeably and say things that are true. If you know what you are talking about, you come across as someone worth listening to. He will not respect your opinion if you are stuttering or rambling about nonsense. You can lose him completely if you say something erroneous, as well.

Get Mad

Usually, when using pessimistic persuasion, you want to come across as the benevolent concerned caretaker. You want to be friendly and warm. But if you are not getting through to someone who is underneath you in status, such as an employee or child, you can use some purposeful anger as a last resort. Get firm and get mad.

You can use threats and tell the person that he is being very stupid. Let him know that he will not be able to recuperate from the losses that he is about to incur. Also let him know that he is hurting everyone and letting everyone down. Don't back down as you say this stuff. Let your anger be righteous. It may just sway him. It will certainly make a serious impression on him.

Be cautious when doing this, however. Only do it when you are dealing with someone who is your inferior and who is resistant to all other measures. You can easily anger someone and even make him want to defy you. Only get angry when you can tell that he will get scared and back down. He must be timid and he must have a lot of respect for you for this to work. In addition, this will only work if you are seldom angry. If you are always acting out in anger, your anger's effects have worn off and will not work as well.

Call on the Past

Do you share history with this person? Do you have mutual memories? Do you have a bond that stretches back into the past, perhaps for years? If so, then you can call on the past to help dissuade someone.

When you are talking someone out of something, you want to make him remember the good times and the good things in his life. Tell him that these good things will end and the future will be bare of them. Let him know that you will miss him and that your heart aches.

When you use pathos, or an emotional appeal, you can easily convince someone not to let go of what he cares about. You can make him realize that he has a good thing and that he is losing it. You are framing a major loss. But this loss is something deeply personal that only you two share. It will have extra special meaning coming from you.

Show Him Gain

We already talked about showing him what he stands to lose. This is usually a great motivator in dissuasion. However, you can also use the process of framing a gain to get someone to change his mind. You want to show him how he will benefit and what he will get if he listens to you. Essentially, you are bribing him with something that he really wants.

You may need to make him a better offer. Find out what he thinks he will gain if he makes this decision. Then offer him better than what he is anticipating. This is a great way to keep customers, who want to switch brands. Find out what they think the other brand offers that is better and then try to top it. Usually, you have to offer them a special bargain or a better rate. This is also a good way to keep a valued employee. Find out what he hopes to gain by quitting and then offer him more money, better benefits, or even a promotion. If someone wants to leave you as a friend or romantic partner, find out what you are doing wrong and work to make it better. You better deliver on your promises, however, or you won't be able to retain a person for very long. He will get tired of waiting for you to change and will eventually go back to the decision that you talked him out of.

You can also offer your subject gains - like how he will earn more recognition and respect if he stays. This could work if someone is trying to give up on a job or something after a trying situation or humiliation. Tell him, "Imagine how much people will look up to you if you don't leave!" or "Maybe if you stick it out, you will earn more respect. People are trying to test you right now. Pass this test by not giving up, and you will be very much admired." Challenge him to stick around to gain more. This could talk him out of his desire to quit and walk away.

Show Him Appreciation

If you show someone how much you love him, depend on him, or appreciate him, you may just satisfy his need to be loved and wanted by others. Then he will feel better about pleasing you. He will choose to do what you want, not what he wants. He will want to continue your approval, so he will work even harder for it.

Remember to tell him thank you when you normally would not. Give him a surprise gift or kiss. Show up to an important event for him, even if you said that you could not make it. Wish him a happy birthday and send a card or a social media message. All of these little gestures show him that you care about him. They make him feel better about your relationship, whatever nature that relationship may be.

Sometimes, a little appreciation is all someone needs to stick around. If you want to keep an employee, friend, lover, or roommate around, consider showing him a little appreciation and thanking him for being there for you. Just this act alone may have a profound effect on changing his mind. People usually don't like change and will avoid it if they can. So if you make it unnecessary for someone to change, then you are golden.

Guilt Trip Him

Guilt is an incredibly powerful emotion. People will do anything to avoid feeling it. You can harness the power of guilt and make someone feel so guilty that he does what you want to avoid the guilt trip. However, be cautious when using a guilt trip, because people hate being guilt tripped. If you do it too often or too much, he will become resentful and resistant to your tricks. The guilt trip is most powerful if only used once when you really need it.

When you guilt trip your subject, you want to find something to make him feel bad about. Keep him from moving by making him feel guilty about leaving behind his aging mother. (This works especially well if you are the aging mother! Moms are great at guilt trips.) Make him feel terrible about taking on more hours by reminding him that quality time with him means everything to his little kids. (This works best if you are the spouse or mother/father of his kids.) Show him that he is hurting you by making his decision so that he chooses to not follow through with that decision in order to avoid hurting you.

The guilt trip usually works best on people who really love you. If you don't have that close of a bond with someone, call on something that you know he cares deeply about, such as his family. Family usually provides the best grounds for a guilt trip. You can also guilt him about his friends or his own health. Some people care enough about these things to feel guilty and do what you want as a result.

When guilt tripping someone, you don't want to act like you are intentionally running a guilt trip. You want to act like a disinterested or hurt third party, making your needs known. If you act like you are doing this deliberately, he will be able to resist your charms better. You don't want that. Instead, pretend to be interested in his well-being and the well-being of those who love him or of yourself. Pretend that you are only pointing out what he is about to hurt or lose with his decision. Avoid telling him that he is selfish and instead just point out what he appears to be forgetting. Guilt trips work best if they are based on genuine hurt.

Chapter 4: Stealthy Pessimistic Persuasion

In most cases, the dissuasion tactics we already discussed are more than sufficient to get someone to change his mind about something. You can talk anyone out of anything with those methods. But in some rare cases, you may not be able to speak to someone directly. For instance, your boss may not want to hear you try to dissuade him from a business decision that you know will end things as you know it at work. In other cases, your best dissuasion attempts simply are not effective and someone refuses to listen to you. What do you do in those circumstances?

Well, under those circumstances, you can start using stealthy pessimistic persuasion. Stealthy pessimistic is secretive, discreet dissuasion. You are dissuading someone using techniques that he cannot recognize. You never become apparent at what you are doing.

Using stealthy pessimistic persuasion is great because you are able to dissuade someone from doing something without ever letting him know what you think or feel. This enables you to gain power over someone because he is not able to resist you. He does not even know what you are doing. He cannot put up a fight or get angry with you. He also cannot find a way to get out of or away from your message, because you are not the one delivering it. At least not directly. He will never know that you are secretly the one delivering the message because you are being as stealthy as a spy.

In addition, stealthy dissuasion works because it leads someone to make his own decision. He will stick to his own decision. He won't feel prideful or controlled, so he will not resist the decision. Meanwhile, the blame is never cast on you. You are out of this. No one will ever guess what hand you played in getting him to change his mind about a decision.

The two most important things about stealthy pessimistic persuasion involve being stealthy and covert, and being persistent. You want to be discreet and never give yourself away. You want to hide what you are really doing. If you overplay your hand and reveal what you are doing, you will drive away your subject and permanently lose his trust. From now on, he will be totally resistant to your persuasion attempts. Using these methods correctly ensures that you continue to appear innocent and uninvolved.

A lot of the methods covered in this chapter are actually subliminal psychological methods. They involve things like classical conditioning. You cannot hope for them to work unless you repeatedly expose your subject to them. You have to be persistent until he finally talks himself out of something. That is when you know that you have been successful and have trained him to make a different choice.

Remember to let your subject do a lot of the work himself. This will be most effective. You don't want to be too involved. You are doing the work here, but you must hide that it is you behind the scenes. View your subject as a puppet, but don't underestimate his intelligence. One slip-up and you can give away what you are really up to. Then it is game over.

Covert Anchors

In persuasion, it is very possible to train someone. When you condition, or train, someone to do what you want, you eliminate the need to use any direct persuasion tactics. Instead, you get this person to do what you want when you expose him to a stimulus. Over time, you can condition someone to act, think, and feel a certain way the minute he hears a noise, sees a color, or smells an aroma. This stimulus is known as a covert anchor. It is an anchor because it brings him to the same feeling every time, leading him to form an association. It is covert because he has no idea why he has made this association and he does not realize that you are actively conditioning him.

This method of classical conditioning can be tweaked a bit to fit pessimistic persuasion. In pessimistic persuasion, you want to create a negative association between a certain thought and a stimulus, so that your subject stops wanting to make whatever decision you want to talk him out of. You must find a negative stimulus to elicit a negative emotion in your subject. Then you must expose him to that stimulus whenever he brings up the topic that you are trying to talk him out of. Some common forms of negative stimulus might include the unpleasant sound of Styrofoam rubbing together, the sound of nails down a chalkboard, the odor of rotten eggs or sewer, a song that brings back bad memories for him, or something else nasty that he hates.

Covert anchors take a while to really set. You need to expose someone to the covert anchor at least a few times to actually form the association that you desire. You cannot just play an ugly stimulus once and expect him to associate it with the topic you are trying to talk him out of. Repeated exposures require some persistence and patience on your part. You need to perform some work to ensure that the association forms. You can tell it has formed when he starts to get a bad feeling about his decision or starts to change his mind.

Covert anchors also are not permanent. They fade with time. You must reaffirm the covert anchor by exposing your subject to it periodically. Otherwise, he will eventually forget the association and your work is wasted. You will have to start all over again. Why waste precious time retraining someone when you can simply keep the training active with periodic exposures?

You don't want to be obvious about this or you will defeat the entire point of stealthy pessimistic persuasion. You don't want to groan whenever someone brings up the topic you don't like, for example, or you will reveal your true feelings and your possible motivation for dissuading someone from something. Rather, you want to be subtle. Let's look at an example to illustrate how to be subtle:

Your husband or wife wants to pick the entire family up and move everyone across the country. You do not want to move and leave your life behind. But you know that your opinion does not matter and your spouse refuses to listen to you or see reason. He or she likes control and won't ever give you an inch. Therefore, whenever your spouse brings up the potential relocation, smile and nod like you agree with it. Then wait a period of time, maybe a few minutes, to ensure that there is some separation between the conversation and your subsequent action. Start playing a song your spouse hates. Maybe bring up the move again as you play this song, to make sure it is still in his or her mind. You don't want to do this right away and make it obvious, but you also don't want to wait so long that your spouse does not create the desired unpleasant association.

Inject an Idea into His Mind

You can inject an idea into someone's mind which will make him eventually change his attitude or stance on something. The best part about this method is that you can appear to be innocent. You can inject the idea without appearing to be doing it deliberately. Your subject will have no idea why suddenly he has a negative association between his idea or decision and some horrible thought, but he will. It may just dissuade him from his path.

You want to inject an idea into your subject's mind very subtly. Once he brings up a decision or starts doing something that you don't like, pretend like you don't care. But then expose him to a shocking and horrible idea.

For instance, your boyfriend or girlfriend has decided to go on a trip out of the country. Act excited for him or her. Then leave a magazine laying around open to an article about disease in the country he wants to go to, or play a clip about a horrific plane crash. The idea will pop into his mind that he might be in mortal danger if he goes on this trip.

Or maybe your spouse wants to move. Agree to it skeptically. Later, play a movie about someone who cannot fit in after a move, or who moves into a haunted house and has no one nearby to help. Even if your spouse does not believe in the paranormal, some part of his mind will realize that things may not be all peachy if he or she decides to move. Maybe staying put is the best course of action.

You can also employ an ally in this method. Have a friend or other third party tell your subject about something horrible so that he loses interest in his decision. For example, have your friend forward him articles about how dangerous overseas travel is. He will think that your friend is the one who is trying to dissuade him and he will not be angry with you for trying to protect him and control him. However, he is also sure to see the idea that you want to inject into his head.

The more people that you can enlist, the stronger the message will be. If he is inundated with bad messages, he may just listen. The bad message is all that he will be able to think about. He may think that the universe is trying to give him some sort of warning or sign not to go through with his plans.

Memories

Memories, particularly emotional memories, are very powerful. They evoke strong emotional responses in people and cause them to make decisions based on their experiences in the past. You can use memories to elicit strong reactions in people and scare them out of decisions.

If your subject is about to do something that you want to dissuade him from, you can subtly remind him of a time period when he made a very similar decision. Remind him of how he failed and suffered. Don't do it in an obvious way. Just bring up the old memories, or reference something else that will remind him of those days.

Say your friend is interested in an investment and you know that it is unwise. When you talk to him about it, he assures you that everything will be just fine because times are different now. Immediately contact an old associate of his who was there when he made a bad investment before and have that old associate of his call him up to catch up. Tell the associate, "Hey, Dave really misses you! You should call him." The associate will unknowingly bring back lots of painful memories for your friend Dave. Dave might just shirk out of the investment after that jaunt down memory lane.

You can also use stimulus that brings back someone's past. Scents and olfactory stimulus are usually best for bringing back memories. Find a perfume of his ex or some other scent that brings back his most unpleasant memories. Make sure that he forms an association with that terrible memory and his current decision.

Lead His Thoughts

While you may want to appear amicable and agreeable on the surface for the sake of stealth, you can still lead someone's thoughts down a certain avenue by using certain language. Your words are harmless so he cannot call you on trying to dissuade him. But the way you use those words can make him hesitate about what he is about to do.

Using positive phrases and light phrases tends to help someone disassociate from bad feelings. For instance, if you are trying to make someone feel less upset about being mugged, you might tell him, "Your wallet was taken," not "Your wallet was stolen." Replace words that carry strong connotations with words that carry less weight. As a result, you will make someone feel better about something.

The reverse is useful in pessimistic persuasion. Instead of sugar coating things with nicer language, create a vaguely unpleasant aura around the topic by using stronger language and more unpleasant phrases. In this case, you would want to say things like "stolen." You want to stir up as many negative images and feelings as possible to make him sour on the idea that he is currently running with.

Don't do this in an obvious way. Rather, be subtle about it. For instance, when he is talking about moving, you might want to tell him that you are satisfied with his decision. He will wonder why you chose that word rather than "happy." Then he will begin to wonder how you really feel about it and if there is something that you are not telling him. He will wonder if there is something you know that he doesn't. This will start to make him feel unsettled about moving.

Show Him What He'll Be Missing

Instead of talking to him about what he will be missing out on, show him. This will come across as more subtle and stealthy. He will not realize what you are really doing. He will just start to realize that maybe he should keep things as they are and not make the change that he is proposing.

You want to start heaping on the love if a person is thinking about leaving your company, town, or marriage. Show him how great things can be. He will remember the good old days and feel sad about leaving. He may decide to stay.

You want to also take him to places that he has fond memories of. Remind him of good memories. Invite him to hang out with old friends that he is sure to miss. Show him the good side of his life or what he is currently doing.

Don't say why you are showing him these things. Just do it. It may make him change his mind in your favor. If you tell him why, however, he may harden his heart to the fond memories and tell you that he is sorry but the past is the past. Let him become overcome with emotion on his own.

Use Subliminal Hints

Subliminal hints are great because they evoke emotional responses and trigger thoughts in someone without you having to do anything. You expose someone to a brief stimulus, something he is not even aware of consciously. This stimulus makes him feel something.

Before someone is about to get on a plane, expose him to a brief flash of an image of a plane crash. He will suddenly be overcome with panic, though he can't place why. Or before someone is about to sign off on a project, slide a piece of paper across his path that says, "Failure." He will suddenly become afraid, even if he didn't really read your note.

Scents are especially useful in subliminal tactics because it is hard for someone to place where a scent is coming from or what it is. You can use a scent that he doesn't like to make him sour toward an idea or decision or to evoke fear in him. For instance, before someone goes on a date, expose her to the scent of her abusive father or even spray that cologne on her date. She will become afraid of him and dislike him.

Hypnotize Your Subject

Hypnosis is an amazing way to gain access to someone's subconscious. Once in his subconscious, you can inject ideas straight into his mind that he will wake up wholeheartedly embracing. He will not be able to argue with or dispel these beliefs once they are planted in his brain.

To perform hypnosis, you want to lull him into a relaxed and receptive state with your words. Use a soft, gentle, monotone voice. Speak to him over and over in the same way until he begins to relax. Go on and on. Tell him to relax if he seems nervous and he will obey your commands if you are dominant in the situation. Once he is relaxed, you can start to ask him to reconsider his decision or commitment. To bring him out of his trance, mention something in the outside world. Say something like, "Look at the time!" He will snap back into awareness and he won't even know why he suddenly feels different and he won't remember what happened to him.

It is even better and easier if you can convince someone to let you hypnotize him. If you have his permission, make him lie down. Guide him into the meditative state by commanding him to sink deeper and deeper into relaxation. You may guide him through an imaginary world, such as a forest or beach, to help him sink into relaxation visually. Only when he is in a trance like state should you begin to ask him if he is sure that his decision is best. Inject the idea of doubt into his mind without being obvious about it. Just asking him if he is certain should be sufficient to stir up doubt in his mind. Further cement that doubt by encouraging him to think about it carefully and guiding him through imagery of what could go wrong if he follows through with his plan. Then slowly begin to bring him out of hypnosis by walking back through the steps of relaxation into wakefulness.

Chapter 5: Using Dissuasion in Psychological Warfare

Thus far, we have discussed pessimistic persuasion, or dissuasion, as a means to get someone to avoid making a decision that hurts you or inconveniences you. We have also considered it as a means to get someone that you care about to make smarter, safer decisions and avoid catastrophe. But now, we can consider it as a means to achieve psychological warfare. Dissuasion can be a powerful weapon that you can use to take your enemies down.

Psychological warfare is the process by which you hurt or defeat someone using purely psychological methods. Psychological warfare is perfectly legal and does not call for violence. Violence is not necessary because you can inflict far greater pain on somebody mentally than physically. A mortal wound will take someone out of his misery; a psychological wound will last forever, creating an ulcer in his self-esteem and hurting him for a long time to come. Therefore, psychological warfare is far better than getting into fist fights with people.

There are two ways that you can use dissuasion to your advantage in psychological warfare. The first way is to dissuade your enemy from doing something that will advance his career or better his life somehow. Make him miss a great opportunity or pass on dating or befriending a truly wonderful person who would make his life brighter. The second way is to talk someone out of helping or pleasing your enemy in order to inconvenience your enemy and strip away his allies. Both methods can be very successful in hindering your enemy's success and hitting him where it counts.

Let's consider a few ways that you can use dissuasion to bruise and batter your enemy without even laying a finger on him. You can use pessimistic persuasion to bring doom and shame into someone's life. This is a powerful weapon, so be careful with it and only use it when you must. You don't want to do irreparable harm to those that you love or your relationship may never recover. Save psychological warfare via dissuasion for your worst enemies or most stubborn and undefeatable opponents in life.

Talk His Best Friends out of Serving Him

Your enemy's most important resource are his allies. Without allies, he cannot do much. A lone wolf does not have half of the power of an army. Therefore, you can disable your enemy and take away his power by turning his allies against him. Strip away the people that he loves and uses for strength to disable him and remove his power. He will not know what to do when he has no allies to lean on for support.

The first way to go about turning his allies against him is to literally turn them against him. Convince them that their friendship with your enemy is no good by telling them about what he does wrong to them. Offer them something better if they join your forces. Make sure that you appeal to a need that your enemy leaves unsatisfied. You might offer his allies better recognition or pleasanter companionship, for example.

You can also start rumors about bad things he said about them or show them his bad side. Expose something ugly or disreputable from his past. Discredit him by making him look like a fool. All of these things can make other people turn against him and stop being friends with him.

The second way to go about this is to stealthily get his allies to not do what he wants, without letting them know what your real motives are. Convince them to take an action other than what your enemy wants them to take. If they are being manipulated too, then they will not even realize that a power struggle is going on between you and your enemy. They will simply let you mess with their minds and sway them whichever way you choose.

For instance, if your enemy is a co-worker and he asks someone to do him a favor to help him gain favor with the boss, convince that person not to do it. Don't say why. Just convince him that it is a bad idea using the methods discussed in this book. Thus, he will not do it and your enemy does not gain that favor that he desired.

You can find little ways to persuade people to not let your enemy get ahead. Dissuade your boss from giving your enemy a raise. Dissuade your friends from ever going out with your enemy. Do what you can to lower his quality of life and irritate him or even hurt him by getting people to not do things for him. You can be stealthy about this and appear like you are not working to destroy your enemy. Secretly, though, you are chipping away at his life and making him miserable.

Hit Him Where it Hurts

Make sure that your moves are strategically planned so that you can hit your enemy wherever it hurts. You can really hurt him if you attack each of his needs, removing one at a time. Remove the things that give him a sense of purpose and higher achievement. Remove the people and friends who love him and make him feel like he belongs. Remove his sense of security, which usually lies in having his familiar environment around him. Remove even his physiological needs, such as food. Make him so uncomfortable that he can't stick around any longer and leaves the job, neighborhood, or wherever it is that he continues to bother you with. Drive him out of your life and claim your territory by removing his needs and debilitating him.

One way to remove his needs is to dissuade people from liking him or helping him. You can do this through a variety of ways. Probably the best way is to subtly slander him. Let something leak, such as an abusive email or some other smear on his character. Make sure the leak cannot be traced back to you. Then, people will come to their own decision to ditch him.

Another way is to ensure that no one ever dates him. You can dissuade people from dating him by telling them what they stand to lose by being around him. If you make him seem unsavory enough, people will scatter and avoid him like the plague. Tell them stories, real or imagined, about how he mistreated all of his exes and his long history with drugs and domestic abuse. Maybe convince people to date you instead if you want to really win the battle with this person.

In the workplace, use persuasion to get your boss to give you all of the important tasks and big projects. Make sure that you get all of the credit for good work. This makes you superior to him. Meanwhile, it tears away his ability to gain recognition for his accomplishments, which can hurt him in his need for recognition and admiration. Lead him to hate work and question his purpose in the company so that he becomes increasingly unhappy at the job. Not only will you be decimating his ego, but you will be removing part of his purpose and his will to live. This can really hurt him where it counts.

Another way to totally decimate your enemy is to dissuade his loved ones from continuing to love him. Break up his family and his marriage. Cause his closest friends to turn against him. People are not as faithful or loyal as they seem. It is surprisingly easy to make people ditch someone that they profess love for. Just expose something shameful or embarrassing about him, and show his loved ones that better is out there and they will elevate themselves in life by moving on.

Pretend to Be a Good Friend

If you really hate someone, your best bet for psychological warfare is to never make your hatred known. Make him think that you like him and are his best friend. Apologize if you have acted coldly or in a hostile manner before and patch things up. Or never let him know that you hate him and wish him evil at all. Treat him with respect and niceness at all times, even if it galls you.

As you do this, you get him to trust you. He lowers his guard. Eventually, he reaches a point where he is willing to take your council. You can then deliberately feed him bad advice and destroy him.

Say that he is thinking about changing jobs. You know that it is a bad idea, so you encourage him to do it. On the other hand, if he wants to change jobs but you happen to know for a fact that his company is about to go under, dissuade him from jumping ships. Use a guilt trip about loyalty to get him to stay with his current company. Then, when he loses everything, you will have successfully hurt him through dissuasion.

You might also dissuade him from other good decisions. When you see that he is about to do something great with his life or make a good decision or seize an excellent opportunity, talk him out of it using the methods outlined earlier.

Convince him to stay safe and secure in what he knows. Poison him with fear so that he refuses to move out of his comfort zone into the unknown. As a result, he will make poor decisions at your council and he will ruin his life. The fault will be his own, too, because he didn't have to listen to you.

Meanwhile, if you are close to him, you can also get close to his family and friends. Poison his image and dissuade everyone from liking him. You can use stealthy pessimistic persuasion in this case so as not to betray your ultimate game. Get people to hate him and cause drama in his life by exposing bad things about him or training people through covert anchors to hate him.

Getting close to your enemies is an excellent psychological warfare tactic. Once you are inside the enemy camp, you can wreak havoc. So try to hide your hatred and convince your enemy that you want the best for him and are a loyal friend. Then you can topple him down.

Use His Loved Ones Against Him

If you notice that some of his loved ones are not happy with him, offer to assist them in getting revenge. Persuade them to team up with you to bring him down. His loved ones will know pertinent information about him. They will also know how to hurt him the worst. Their betrayal will cause him to suffer huge blows to his ego.

You don't always need to do a lot of work to dissuade someone from being with your enemy. All you have to do is be observant. If someone is unhappy with your enemy, then exploit that immediately. Show the person what he or she stands to gain by bringing your enemy down with you. He or she will make the decision quickly enough. You can promise revenge as a gain; this is often sufficient if someone that he is close to is bitter or estranged.

You can also turn his loved ones against him by dissuading him from doing something important, thus making them angry with him. Let's consider an example of this complex but beautiful tactic. Your co-worker seems to feel guilty about going out for drinks and insists that he gets home to his wife. So you convince him to stay for a few more rounds. You use a guilt trip to make him feel bad about leaving, so he stays a little later. In that time frame, you get him trashed. One thing leads to another, until he ends up home very late. His wife is now furious with him. You just managed to create conflict and stress in his life without even speaking to his wife.

Look for similar opportunities to this to dissuade your enemy from doing what he should do to keep his loved ones happy with him. Then, you can make his loved ones dole out the most hurt. After all, sharp words from his wife will cut him far more deeply than sharp words from you. His loved ones can hurt him much more than you can. So use them as tools and let their natural drama play out.

Every family or friend group has its own unique dynamic and set of problems. If you observe a group or family long enough, their issues start to become apparent. You can see who is jealous of whom and who craves more attention and who must always win or be right. Then you can play these dynamics by getting your enemy to do the one thing he should not do. Have him set off his family's anger by dissuading him from taking an action or doing something that he should do for them.

Dissuade Him from Attacking You

A crucial part of every type of warfare is strategic self-defense. You cannot hope to win if you do not have a defense strategy in place. You must be able to stick up for yourself when you are fighting with someone. This is another way that dissuasion can come into play.

When your enemy tries to fight with you or come at you with a psychological attack, you can dissuade him from hurting you. You can talk him out of fighting with you and convince him to accept you as an ally rather than an enemy. Show him that he will gain more if he works with you rather than fighting you. Of course, you could be lying. You may have no interest in establishing peace with your enemy. But pretending to be his friend and getting him to drop his attack is a good strategy for defending yourself.

On the other hand, you can remain enemies, but get him to stop fighting with you by showing him what he stands to lose by going up against you. Intimidate him before he even makes a move. Frame the loss that he will sustain if he loses against you. Let him know how many friends you have and why he does not stand a chance against you. Bluff if you have to. The more confident you come across, the more intimidating you will be. He will not be able to tell if you are wearing a poker face or not, so he will get scared and give up instead of risking it.

Conclusion

Now you have read all about pessimistic persuasion. You have learned about how to talk anyone out of anything. Do you feel better about your persuasion skills? You should because now you know all of the tools necessary for pessimistic persuasion.

You first must keep the basic concepts of persuasion in mind. Take a cue from Dr. Robert Cialdini, the leading expert in influence psychology. You must get someone to want to do what you want – even if that means getting someone to change his mind about something. You must make him think that something is scarce so that he jumps at it. You must also convince him to like you and to trust you as an authority figure that he should listen to. Finally, you must get him to feel that he owes you. There are many ways that you can use these Six Principles of Influence, so you should have unlimited options as to how you can influence someone.

You also must focus on satisfying someone's needs, using the Maslow Hierarchy of Needs. A person won't do what you say just because you want it. You must make him want to do it by promising him a reward that he actually wants. Satisfying one of his main needs is a good way to go about doing this. Most people want to be liked and recognized for their accomplishments, so you can usually rely on those needs and promise someone friends or esteem in exchange for their actions.

There are various other tricks to persuasion, but the main concept that they all share in common is appealing to someone. You must be sympathetic, kind, and trustworthy. You must come across as warm and likable. And above all, you must find some way to motivate a person to do what you want. Motivational methods can include challenging someone, using reverse psychology on someone, or even just baiting him with the promise of something that he would want. You have to motivate someone to do what you want, or persuasion won't work. Make an appealing offer and someone will take it.

When using pessimistic persuasion, all of these basic persuasion tactics work just as well. You just have to tailor them to fit your cause. You are probably trying to get someone to see that you are right and take your advice. Therefore, you want to make an appeal to the person's intelligence or heart. Meanwhile, you want to prove that you are an authority that the person should listen to and trust.

You can't just force your opinion on someone to talk him out of something. Doing so will put him on the defensive and cause him to reject what you have to say. Being right is not as important as convincing him that your opinion is better. Therefore, don't create an argument that you are bent on winning. Rather, work to coax him into seeing the wisdom of your point of view.

Show him that there are more benefits for him if he changes his mind, than if he sticks with it.

Sometimes, people refuse to see logic. If your subject is bent on getting his way, then you should switch to more stealthy methods of persuasion. Get him to change his mind on his own through subtle hints and subliminal stimulus. Stealthy pessimistic persuasion is best only used when you are up against someone who is totally resistant to your ideas.

Usually, it is best to use more direct methods of persuasion. Only whip out the conditioning or subliminal stimulus when you must. You don't want to ever get caught using these methods, or your subject will never trust you again and will become exceptionally resistant to your persuasion attempts. The whole idea behind stealthy persuasion is never getting caught. Use stealth when executing your methods. If you execute them correctly, you will never, ever be found out. Your subject will never even guess that you are the reason why he suddenly has a change of heart.

In fact, most forms of persuasion are useful only when direct appeals don't work. The minute someone tells you no, you must work to change his mind. You can't always do this by pleading with him directly. Obviously he wants to do what you don't want. You can only get him to come around to your point of view and change his mind if you make him see that your option is the best option. It is not always necessary to show him that this option is your idea; you will enjoy more success if you let him think that it's his idea instead.

Persuasion is not necessarily easy. There is always the risk that you will say the wrong thing or that you will fail to be convincing enough. But when persuasion fails, you can always try other tactics. The more you practice persuasion, the better you will become at it. Pessimistic persuasion is certainly difficult to accomplish, but it is worth it. You can talk someone out of a bad decision or you can argue with your boss to keep your job. It can prove to be lifesaving.

Now that you know how to perform pessimistic persuasion, you are set to talk anyone out of anything. You can easily start to make your life better by being able to sway people to do what you want and not what you don't want. Use this skill wisely.

Thank you for reading.